REC
from
VINEYARDS
of
NORTHERN
CALIFORNIA

VEGETARIAN
Dishes

Leslie Mansfield

CELESTIALARTS
Berkeley, California

When preparing recipes that call for egg yolks or whites, whether or not they are to be cooked, use only the highest-quality, salmonella-free eggs.

CELESTIALARTS
P.O. Box 7123
Berkeley, California 94707

Distributed in Canada by Ten Speed Canada, in the United Kingdom and Europe by Airlift Books, in New Zealand by Southern Publishers Group, in Australia by Simon & Schuster Australia, in South Africa by Real Books, and in Singapore, Malaysia, Hong Kong, and Thailand by Berkeley Books.

Cover and interior design by Greene Design
Cover photograph by Larry Kunkel
Photo styling by Veronica Randall
Public Domain Art thanks to Dover Publications

Library of Congress Card Catalog Number 00-131956

First printing, 2000
Printed in the United States

1 2 3 4 5 6 7—04 03 02 01 00

To my niece
JENNA,
who sparkles when she helps me bake.

ACKNOWLEDGMENTS

Deepest gratitude goes to my husband, Richard, who has helped me with every step—his name belongs on the title page along with mine. To my wonderful parents, Stewart and Marcia Whipple, for their unflagging confidence. To Phil Wood, who makes dreams a reality. To my dear friend and editor Veronica Randall, whose creativity, intelligence, and wit make working with Celestial Arts a joy. To Victoria Randall, for her invaluable assistance. To Brad Greene, for another spectacular design. To Larry Kunkel, for his glorious photography.

Finally, this book would not have been possible without the cooperation of all our friends at the wineries who graciously contributed their favorite recipes. I wish to thank them all for their generosity.

Table of Contents

Introduction

Just mention California wine country and thoughts of warm sunshine, vines heavy with ripening grapes, and a relaxed lifestyle come to mind. The small villages throughout the wine country each have their own personalities, as do the wineries. From rural, family-run boutique wineries to large, stately wineries surrounded by a sea of vineyards, they all have one thing in common—a love for good food and wine.

This love of food and wine has resulted in an explosion of cutting-edge ideas that have defined California cuisine, incorporating the finest of Europe and Asia while drawing on the incredible local and seasonal bounty.

Entertaining is a way of life in wine country. Whether it is a formal dinner with many courses to showcase a variety of wines, or just drawing off a pitcher of new wine from the barrel to go with an impromptu picnic with neighbors, the desire to share the best they have to offer has helped shape the cuisine of California.

In the following pages you will find recipes offered from the finest wineries of Northern California. Each is a reflection of their personality, whether formal or casual, and all are delicious. Each one is a taste of wine country.

1

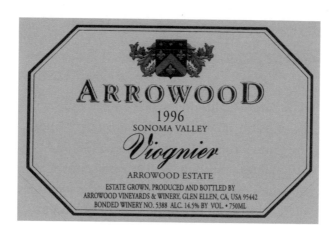

ARROWOOD VINEYARDS AND WINERY

Richard Arrowood, one of California's most renowned winemakers, and his wife and partner, Alis Demers Arrowood, have crafted a winery that sits in perfect harmony with its environs. Fashioned after a New England farmhouse, the winery has often been described as a "winemaker's dream." Home to a number of wonderful, rare, and outstanding wines, Arrowood uses an intimate knowledge of the Sonoma Valley's many microclimates and terroirs to create great and complex wines.

GREEK EGGPLANT & FETA PURÉE

This is a wonderful side dish, or, when served with pita bread, it makes a satisfying lunch.

2 eggplants

Juice of 1 lemon

1/4 cup butter

2 tablespoons all-purpose flour

1 cup milk

1 cup crumbled feta cheese

Salt and freshly ground black pepper to taste

Minced fresh parsley

Preheat oven to 375 degrees F.

Place both whole eggplants on a baking sheet. Roast for 20 to 30 minutes, or until the skin is blackened and the eggplants are very soft. When cool enough to handle, cut off the stem end, then slice into quarters lengthwise. Place, skin side down, on a cutting board. With the back of a knife, scrape the flesh off the skin. Discard the skin.

In the bowl of a food processor, combine the eggplant flesh and lemon juice. Process until smooth, then set aside.

(recipe continued on next page)

In a saucepan, melt the butter over medium heat. Whisk in the flour until smooth and bubbly. Slowly whisk in the milk. Continue to cook, whisking constantly, until thickened. Reduce the heat to low and whisk in eggplant pureé. Simmer for about 20 minutes, whisking often, until the mixture has thickened.

Add the feta cheese and whisk until smooth. Season with salt and pepper. Simmer about 5 minutes, or until heated through. Divide onto plates and sprinkle with parsley.

Serves 4 to 6
Serve with Arrowood Vineyards and Winery Viognier

Wine makes daily living easier, less hurried, with fewer tensions and more tolerance.

Benjamin Franklin

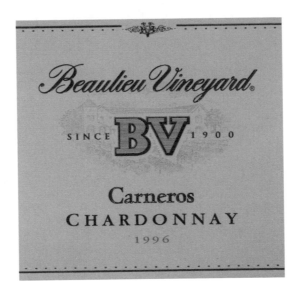

BEAULIEU VINEYARD

Beaulieu Vineyard (BV) was founded in 1900 by Frenchman Georges de Latour, who came from a winegrowing family in Bordeaux. Since its inception, BV has been an important player in the history of California winemaking. Under the guidance of legendary winemaker Andre Techelistcheff, beginning in 1938, BV's famous Georges de Latour Cabernet Sauvignon Private Reserve set the standard for California Cabernet through the rest of the century. Madame de Latour, who ran the company in the 1940s, was a brilliant and outspoken promoter of BV and even had the audacity to show her family's wines in her native France, and won over her countrymen. BV has been a major pioneer of the cool Carneros district of Napa, now legendary for fine Pinot Noir and Chardonnay. The winery is now owned by United Distillers and Vintners North America, and current winemaker Joel Aiken continues the great tradition along with the fine sense of innovation established by Georges de Latour and Andre Techelistcheff.

CHANTERELLE & ROASTED GARLIC BREAD PUDDING

The heady aroma of the chanterelles would balance nicely with a juicy roast.

2 whole heads garlic

1/4 cup olive oil

Salt and freshly ground black pepper to taste

2 cups milk

4 eggs

1 teaspoon thyme

1/2 teaspoon white pepper

3 tablespoons butter

8 ounces chanterelle mushrooms, sliced

1/2 loaf day-old French bread, cut into 1-inch cubes and lightly toasted

1 cup grated Romano cheese

Preheat oven to 250 degrees F.

Remove the papery outer skins from the garlic, leaving whole heads intact. Slice 1/4 inch off the top. Place in a small baking dish and drizzle with olive oil. Season with salt and pepper. Bake for about 2 hours, basting occasionally, until the garlic is very tender. Remove from the oven and cool. Squeeze the garlic from the skins into the bowl of a food processor. Add the milk, eggs, thyme, and white pepper and process until smooth. Season with salt and set aside.

In a skillet, melt the butter over medium heat. Add the mushrooms and sauté until just tender.

Increase oven temperature to 325 degrees F. Butter a $2^1/2$-quart baking dish.

Spread half the toasted bread in the bottom of prepared baking dish. Follow with half the sautéed mushrooms, and sprinkle with half of the Romano cheese. Repeat with the remaining bread, mushrooms, and cheese. Pour the milk mixture over the top and press to submerge all ingredients. Let stand 30 minutes. Bake for 50 to 60 minutes, or until the custard is set and the top is golden brown.

Serves 6
Serve with Beaulieu Vineyard
Chardonnay

ATLAS PEAK VINEYARDS

Atlas Peak Vineyards is situated in an uplifted, hanging valley 1,450 to 1,800 feet above sea level in the Vaca Mountain range that forms the eastern rim of Napa Valley. Within this subappellation of the Napa Valley, 500 acres of mountain vineyards have been planted to Cabernet Sauvignon, Sangiovese, and Chardonnay.

A joint venture between Allied Domecq Wines and Piero Antinori, whose family has a 600-year winegrowing history in Italy, Atlas Peak Vineyards has made the production of Sangiovese their specialty and is now the leading producer of this noble variety in the United States. This venerable grape, from the Tuscan region of Italy, exhibits delicate aromas and structured tannins and is the wine upon which the cuisine of Tuscany is based.

SAUTÉED GREENS

*Use beet tops, Swiss chard, or collards for this
healthful dish from Heidi Cusick.*

1 tablespoon olive oil

1 shallot, minced

1 pound greens, cut into strips

2 cloves garlic, minced

1/4 cup water

2 tablespoons soy sauce

1/2 teaspoon cayenne

Salt and freshly ground black pepper to taste

🌿 In a large skillet, heat the olive oil over medium-
high heat. Add the shallot and sauté until tender.
Add the greens and the garlic. Pour in the water,
cover, and simmer about 15 minutes, stirring often,
until tender. Remove the lid and simmer until most
of the liquid has evaporated. Stir in the soy sauce,
cayenne, salt, and pepper. Serve immediately.

Serves 4
Serve with Atlas Peak Vineyards
Sangiovese

BELVEDERE VINEYARDS
AND WINERY

In Italian, "belvedere" means "beautiful view," which aptly describes the vista from this rustic redwood winery in the Russian River Valley. The winery was built in 1982, the same year owners Bill and Sally Hambrecht bought their first piece of vineyard land high atop Bradford Mountain in Dry Creek Valley. Over the years they purchased and planted additional estate vineyards in the Dry Creek, Alexander, and Russian River Valleys in northern Sonoma County. As Bill Hambrecht often says, "Our most valuable asset is our vineyards. Good vineyards are as valuable as gold to a winery, and Belvedere has access to some of Sonoma County's best."

ROASTED CHILE DIP

Bring this savory dip, tortilla chips, and a bottle of Belvedere Merlot to your next get-together.

6 Anaheim chiles

3 tablespoons olive oil

1 onion, finely chopped

1 clove garlic, minced

1 cup dark beer

1 cup (8 ounces) queso fresco (Mexican mild cheese), grated

1/2 cup (4 ounces) cheddar cheese, grated

1/2 cup sour cream

1/2 teaspoon salt

1/4 teaspoon freshly ground black pepper

Preheat oven to 450 degrees F. Lightly oil a baking sheet.

Brush the chiles with 1 tablespoon of the olive oil and place on the prepared baking sheet. Roast the chiles for 25 to 30 minutes, or until blackened. Remove from the oven and place the hot chiles in a plastic bag. Let them steam in the bag until cool. Remove the skins and seeds and discard. Chop the chiles and set aside.

(recipe continued on next page)

Reduce the oven temperature to 350 degrees F. Lightly oil a 1^1/2-quart baking dish.

In a skillet, heat the remaining olive oil over medium heat. Add the onion and sauté until tender. Add the garlic and reserved chiles and sauté until fragrant. Pour in the beer, lower the heat, and simmer until most of the liquid has evaporated. Remove from heat and transfer the chile mixture to a large bowl.

Stir in the queso fresco, cheddar cheese, sour cream, salt, and pepper until well blended. Transfer the mixture to the prepared baking dish. Bake for 25 minutes, or until hot and bubbly.

Serves 6 to 8
Serve with Belvedere Vineyards and Winery Merlot

BENZIGER FAMILY WINERY

The Benziger Family, producers of Benziger Family, Reserve, and Imagery Wines, believes that the nature of great wine lies in the vineyard's character, the winemaker's artistry, and the family's passion. At Benziger this means farming and vinifying select vineyards to mine the unique character of each, winemaking that combines intuition and artistry with a minimalist philosophy, and passion that is shared by the entire family. In its quest for uniqueness through diversity, the family produces over 300 lots of grapes each year from more than 60 ranches, in more than a dozen appellations.

PORTABELLA MUSHROOMS *Stuffed with Eggplant & Gorgonzola*

This simple but spectacular recipe was inspired by my friend Paul Willis.

4 portabella mushrooms, cleaned

Salt and freshly ground black pepper to taste

3 tablespoons olive oil

1 eggplant, peeled and cut into 1/4-inch cubes

4 sun-dried tomato halves in oil, finely chopped

2 cloves garlic, minced

1/4 cup Benziger Family Winery Cabernet Franc

4 ounces Gorgonzola cheese, crumbled

1/2 cup freshly grated Parmesan cheese

Preheat oven to 375 degrees F. Lightly oil a rimmed baking sheet.

With a small sharp knife, carefully cut out the tough mushroom stems and discard. Place the mushrooms, gill side up, on the prepared baking sheet. Sprinkle with salt and pepper. Set aside.

In a large skillet, heat the olive oil over medium heat. Add the eggplant and sauté until very tender and lightly browned. Add the sun-dried tomatoes and garlic and sauté until fragrant. Stir in the wine and continue to cook until the liquid has evaporated. Transfer the eggplant mixture to a bowl. Stir in the Gorgonzola and season with salt and pepper.

Divide the filling between the mushrooms, spreading the filling evenly onto each mushroom. Loosely tent the mushrooms with aluminum foil and bake for 15 minutes. Remove the foil and bake an additional 15 minutes, or until the cheese is melted and the mushrooms are tender. Serve immediately.

Serves 4
Serve with Benziger Family Winery
Cabernet Franc

BUENA VISTA WINERY

Buena Vista Winery, located near the town of Sonoma, was built in 1857 by the storied Hungarian Count Agoston Haraszthy. Known as the "father of California viticulture," Count Haraszthy, after constructing Buena Vista's stone winery and underground cellars, traveled to Europe on a mission to bring back cuttings of European grape vines. These vines, from the greatest vineyards of France, became the source for much of California's early vineyard plantings.

Over a century later, in 1979, the Moller-Racke family of Germany purchased the winery and invested in prime vineyard land within the Carneros region. Today, Buena Vista is the largest estate winery in Carneros.

RIGATONI
with RICOTTA

This rustic tomato-sauced pasta was created for Buena Vista by the well-known cookbook author Janet Fletcher.

3 cups ripe Roma tomatoes, peeled, seeded, and chopped

2 tablespoons olive oil

2 cloves garlic, thinly sliced

1/4 teaspoon hot red chile flakes

2 teaspoons minced fresh oregano

Salt to taste

1/8 teaspoon sugar

1 pound rigatoni pasta, cooked in boiling salted water until al dente, then drained

4 ounces fresh whole-milk ricotta cheese, at room temperature

2 tablespoons minced parsley

Freshly grated Parmesan cheese

(recipe continued on next page)

🦋 Place the tomatoes in the bowl of a food processor and purée until smooth. Set aside.

In a large skillet, heat the olive oil over medium-low heat. Add the garlic and sauté until fragrant. Add the red chile flakes and sauté briefly to release their fragrance. Add the puréed tomatoes and oregano. Add the salt and sugar. Cook, stirring occasionally, until the sauce is thick and smooth, about 15 minutes.

Transfer the drained hot pasta to a large bowl. Add the sauce, ricotta, and parsley. Toss until the ricotta melts and the pasta is evenly coated with sauce. Transfer to warm plates and sprinkle with Parmesan. Serve immediately.

Serves 4
Serve with Buena Vista Winery
Pinot Noir

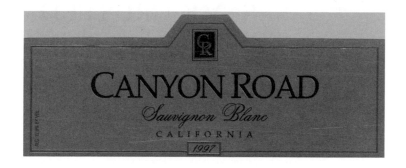

CANYON ROAD WINERY

One of Sonoma County's more picturesque settings, Canyon Road Winery is a favorite among wine country visitors. A warm and friendly tasting room features award-winning Canyon Road wines, including some limited selections available only at the winery. Visitors can enjoy a country deli and gift shop, picnic areas by the vines, complimentary wine tasting, and great hospitality.

SPICY BLACK & WHITE SESAME-CRUSTED TOFU *with Baby Bok Choy*

Plain white rice is a perfect foil for this flavorful dish.

1 pound extra-firm tofu

3 tablespoons sake

3 tablespoons soy sauce

2 tablespoons sesame oil

2 tablespoons hoisin sauce

1 1/2 tablespoons salted black beans, rinsed and minced

1 teaspoon sambal oelek

2 tablespoons black sesame seeds

2 tablespoons white sesame seeds

3 tablespoons vegetable oil

4 cloves garlic, minced

4 baby bok choy, cut in half lengthwise

Slice the tofu crosswise into 8 pieces. Drain on paper towels. In a shallow dish, stir together the sake, soy sauce, sesame oil, hoisin sauce, black beans, and sambal oelek. Place the tofu in the dish, cover, and marinate in the refrigerator for 2 hours or overnight. Remove the tofu from the marinade and drain briefly. Reserve excess marinade.

Place the sesame seeds on a plate. Dip the tofu into sesame seeds and press lightly to coat one side. In a large skillet, heat the vegetable oil over medium heat. Cook the tofu, sesame seed side down, for about 3 minutes or until golden brown. Turn and cook on the other side until golden brown. Transfer to a plate and keep warm.

Add the garlic to the skillet and sauté until fragrant. Add the bok choy and cook until lightly browned on both sides. Stir in the reserved marinade, and simmer just until the bok choy is tender. Divide the bok choy onto 4 plates and top with 2 pieces of tofu. Drizzle pan juices over the top and serve immediately.

Serves 4
Serve with Canyon Road Winery
Sauvignon Blanc

CARDINALE WINERY

Cardinale Rule: Make grape selection an obsession and gentle winemaking a virtue. Grow fruit of intense vineyard and varietal character from the finest sites in the Mayacamas. Pick only when the fruit is physiologically ripe and balanced in flavor. Hand harvest into small lug boxes, during the cool of the morning. Keep each vineyard separate, in order to know it better. Hand sort all fruit and use only sound, ripe berries. Carefully crack the berries and begin native yeast fermentation. Let juice and skins macerate gently for 25 to 35 days to maximize flavor and texture. Use a traditional basket press to deepen midpalate flavors. Place into 100% new tight-grained French oak château barrels. Attentively rack wine from barrel to barrel every three months. Age in barrel for 18 to 21 months. Bottle unfiltered. Age in bottle for 12 months before release. Enjoy, or bottle age for an additional 5 to 10 years.

GARDEN NAPOLEONS *with* *Roasted Red Pepper Sauce*

These beautiful and succulent treats showcase the Cardinale Royale to perfection.

ROASTED RED PEPPER SAUCE:

2 red bell peppers, cut in half and seeded

2 tablespoons olive oil

2 teaspoons freshly squeezed lemon juice

1 eggplant, cut crosswise into 8 slices

2 zucchini, cut in half lengthwise, then cut in half crosswise

1 onion, cut into 8 slices

2 tomatoes, cut into 4 thick slices

1/4 cup olive oil

Salt and freshly ground black pepper to taste

8 ounces fresh mozzarella, cut into 8 slices

2 tablespoons minced fresh Italian parsley

 **For the sauce:** Preheat oven to 450 degrees F. Lightly oil a baking sheet.

(recipe continued on next page)

Brush the bell peppers with the olive oil and place on the prepared baking sheet. Roast the peppers for about 30 minutes or until blackened. Remove from oven and place the hot peppers in a plastic bag. Let them steam in the bag until cool. Remove the skins and discard. Place the red bell peppers in a blender with the lemon juice and purée. Place in a bowl and set aside.

Reduce oven temperature to 400 degrees F. Lightly oil 2 baking sheets.

Place the vegetable slices in one layer on the baking sheets. Brush with olive oil and season with salt and pepper. Roast for about 20 minutes, or until lightly browned. Remove from the oven and let cool.

To assemble the Napoleons: Place a slice of eggplant on a baking sheet. Top with a slice of zucchini, then onion, mozzarella, eggplant, tomato, and mozzarella. Sprinkle with parsley. Repeat with the remaining ingredients to make 4 Napoleons. Reduce oven temperature to 350 degrees F. Bake for 10 minutes, or until the cheese has softened. Divide the sauce onto 4 plates and place a Napoleon on top. Serve immediately.

Serves 4
Serve with Cardinale Winery
Royale

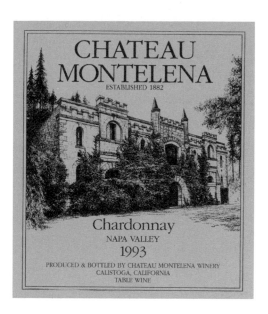

CHATEAU MONTELENA WINERY

A visit to Chateau Montelena is a must for wine lovers seeking excellence. With thick natural stone walls, which maintain perfect temperature and humidity for aging wine, and the exceptional grapes that come from their Estate Vineyard, Chateau Montelena has earned its reputation as one of California's first growths. Even the French, for the first time in the history of winemaking, named the Chateau Montelena Chardonnay the world's greatest Chardonnay in 1976.

PUMPKIN RISOTTO

Arborio, the classic risotto rice, lends a heavenly creaminess while keeping its al dente texture.

1 pound sugar pumpkin, cut in half

1 tablespoon butter

1 tablespoon olive oil

1 leek, pale green part only, finely chopped

1 clove garlic, minced

1 cup Arborio rice

1/2 cup Chateau Montelena Winery Chardonnay

2 1/2 cups vegetable stock

1/2 cup heavy cream

1/4 cup freshly grated Parmesan cheese

1 tablespoon minced fresh sage

Salt and freshly ground black pepper to taste

Preheat oven to 400 degrees F. Lightly oil a rimmed baking sheet.

Place the pumpkin, cut side down, on the prepared baking sheet. Roast the pumpkin for about 30 minutes, or until tender when pierced with a skewer. Remove from the oven and let cool. Remove the peel and discard. Cut the pumpkin into

¹/4-inch cubes, and set aside 8 ounces of the diced pumpkin. Keep the remainder for another use.

In a large saucepan, heat the butter and olive oil over medium heat. Add the leek and garlic and sauté until tender. Stir in the rice and sauté until the rice begins to turn light golden brown. Stir in the wine and sauté until the liquid has almost evaporated.

In a saucepan, bring the vegetable stock to a simmer over medium-low heat. Ladle enough simmering stock into the rice to just cover the rice. Lower the heat under the rice to medium-low and stir constantly until the rice has almost absorbed all of the liquid. Add more simmering stock to just cover the rice and continue stirring until almost absorbed. Repeat this process until the rice is tender but still firm. This will take about 20 minutes. Stir in the cream, Parmesan, and sage until the rice absorbs most of the liquid and the mixture is creamy. Stir in the reserved pumpkin and season with salt and pepper. Serve immediately.

Serves 4 to 6
Serve with Château Montelena Winery
Chardonnay

DE LOACH
VINEYARDS

The morning fog along the Russian River Valley, a product of marine influence, is instrumental for the quality of Cecil and Christine De Loach's estate-grown wines. This cooling influence in the heat of late summer allows their vines to fully develop their fruit while maintaining acidity and elegance. Cecil and Christine De Loach's personal connection to their vineyards and cellar ensures a consistency of style and excellence in quality year after year.

SALAD OF BABY GREENS *with Toasted Pine Nut Vinaigrette*

This simple yet sublimely seasoned salad will whet the appetite for the meal to come.

²/3 cup pine nuts

¹/2 cup olive oil

3 tablespoons white wine vinegar

¹/2 teaspoon salt

¹/2 teaspoon tarragon

¹/8 teaspoon freshly grated nutmeg

³/4 teaspoon finely minced lemon zest

White pepper

1¹/2 pounds mixed baby greens

Preheat oven to 350 degrees F.

Spread the pine nuts on a baking sheet. Bake for about 5 minutes, or until lightly toasted. Let cool.

In a bowl, whisk together the olive oil, vinegar, salt, tarragon, and nutmeg. Whisk in the lemon zest and white pepper. Toss the dressing with baby greens and divide onto 6 plates. Spoon the pine nuts on top.

Serves 6
Serve with De Loach Vineyards Russian River Valley Chardonnay

DOMAINE CARNEROS

Designed after Château de la Marquetterie in Champagne, with its roots in the French house of Taittinger, Domaine Carneros is the only sparkling wine producer using exclusively Carneros grapes for their super-premium méthode-champenoise. Situated atop a knoll surrounded by its vineyards, the château commands a spectacular view of the rolling hills of Carneros. Pinot Noir and Chardonnay, along with a lesser amount of Pinot Meunier, serve as the basis of Domaine Carneros's elegant and delicate sparkling wines.

PEAR, TARRAGON & GRUYÈRE SOUFFLÉ

This delicate soufflé, from chef Bryan Page, would be the basis of a quintessential romantic dinner.

1 1/4 cups peeled and diced pears

3/4 cup Domaine Carneros Sparkling Wine

1 teaspoon sugar

3 tablespoons butter, softened

3 tablespoons all-purpose flour

1/2 cup milk

1 cup grated Gruyère cheese

1 1/2 tablespoons minced fresh tarragon

1/2 teaspoon salt

1/8 teaspoon white pepper

1/8 teaspoon freshly grated nutmeg

4 egg yolks

5 egg whites

1/4 teaspoon cream of tartar

(recipe continued on next page)

🍃 Preheat oven to 375 degrees F. Butter a 2-quart soufflé dish.

In a saucepan, combine the pears, wine, and sugar. Cook over medium heat until the pears are very tender. Purée the pear mixture and set aside.

In a saucepan, melt the butter over medium heat. Whisk in the flour until smooth. Cook the mixture until bubbly. Lower the heat and slowly whisk in the milk. Simmer, whisking constantly, until the mixture thickens. Remove from the heat and whisk in $3/4$ cup of the cheese until melted. Whisk in reserved the pear pureé, tarragon, salt, white pepper, and nutmeg. Whisk in the egg yolks.

In a bowl, beat the egg whites until stiff. Beat in the cream of tartar. Gently but thoroughly fold the egg whites into the pear mixture, taking care not to deflate the egg whites. Pour the mixture into the prepared soufflé dish. Sprinkle with the remaining cheese. Bake for 25 to 30 minutes, or until golden brown. Remove from oven and serve immediately.

Serves 4 to 6
Serve with Domaine Carneros
Sparkling Wine

DUCKHORN
VINEYARDS

When your last name is Duckhorn, it stands to reason that you would choose a duck to be a symbol for your winery. Dan and Margaret Duckhorn have taken that theme and created one of the Napa Valley's most respected premium wineries. Hand harvested and sorted grapes enter their crusher to emerge as ultra-premium Cabernets, Merlots, Zinfandels, and Sauvignon Blancs. New vineyards in Mendocino's Anderson Valley promise to deliver world-class Pinot Noirs to their flock of stylistic wines.

TUSCAN
WHITE BEANS
Simmered in Wine

A hearty main course for a luncheon or dinner.

8 ounces dried white beans

1 cup Duckhorn Vineyards Sauvignon Blanc

1/3 cup olive oil

5 Roma tomatoes, peeled, seeded, and chopped

1 onion, finely chopped

1 carrot, finely chopped

2 tablespoons minced fresh Italian parsley

1 clove garlic, minced

Salt and freshly ground black pepper to taste

Freshly grated Parmesan cheese

Rinse the beans in cold water. Place the beans in a bowl and cover with plenty of cold water. Let stand overnight.

The next day, pour the beans and their soaking liquid into a large saucepan. Bring to a boil, then reduce heat to medium-low, and simmer for 1 hour. Drain the beans in a colander, then return the beans to the pan. Add the wine, olive oil, tomatoes, onion, carrot, parsley, and garlic and bring to a boil. Reduce the heat to medium-low, cover the saucepan, and simmer for about 1½ hours, or until the beans are very tender. Remove the lid and season with salt and pepper. Continue to simmer for about 30 minutes, or until the liquid is reduced by half, and the beans are thick. Divide into 4 bowls and sprinkle with Parmesan.

Serves 4
Serve with Duckhorn Vineyards
Sauvignon Blanc

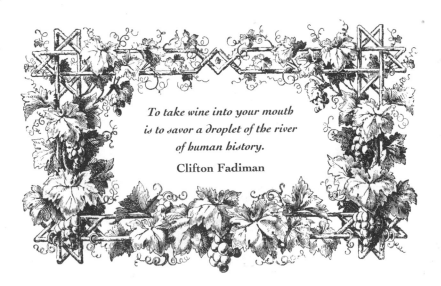

To take wine into your mouth is to savor a droplet of the river of human history.

Clifton Fadiman

DRY CREEK VINEYARD

Dry Creek Vineyard was the first new winery to be established in the Dry Creek Valley of Sonoma after Prohibition. Synonymous with fine winemaking, Dry Creek Vineyard draws upon over 35 different vineyards to produce their wines, matching the particular soils and microclimates of each site to the varieties that do best in the Dry Creek Valley.

FUMÉ
TOMATO BRIE

Serve as an appetizer when special friends arrive.

1 wheel of Brie cheese, 8 inches in diameter

1/4 cup olive oil

1/4 cup finely chopped shallots

2 cloves garlic, chopped

1 cup chopped sun-dried tomatoes (not oil-packed)

1 cup Dry Creek Vineyard Fumé Blanc

Salt and freshly ground black pepper to taste

2 tablespoons capers

French bread

Preheat oven to 350 degrees F. Lightly oil a
1-quart baking dish.

Place the Brie in the prepared baking dish and bake
for about 20 minutes, or until soft and runny. Check
during the last few minutes to prevent burning.

In a saucepan, heat the olive oil over medium heat.
Add the shallots and garlic and sauté until transparent.
Stir in the tomatoes and wine and simmer until the
sauce has thickened. Season with salt and pepper.

Remove Brie from oven and pour the sauce over it.
Sprinkle capers on top. Serve with crusty French bread.

Serves 6
Serve with Dry Creek Vineyard
Fumé Blanc

FERRARI-CARANO VINEYARDS AND WINERY

Villa Fiore, or "House of Flowers," at Ferrari-Carano is one of the most spectacular wineries and visitors' centers in the northern California wine country. Designed to reflect the proud Italian heritage of the Carano family, Villa Fiore houses state-of-the-art kitchens, which are used to educate professionals as well as consumers in the enjoyment of Ferrari-Carano wines. Ferrari-Carano draws its grapes from fourteen winery-owned vineyards over a 50-mile area, from Alexander Valley in the north to the Carneros district in the south. This exceptional supply of fruit allows the winemaker to produce the highly stylized wines for which Ferrari-Carano is known.

SALAD *with Gorgonzola, Golden Raisins & Toasted Pine Nuts*

*The flavors of the Mediterranean come alive
in this fresh and sprightly salad.*

3/4 cup golden raisins

1/2 cup Ferrari-Carano Winery Fumé Blanc Reserve

6 cups torn butter lettuce

2/3 cup olive oil

1/3 cup balsamic vinegar

Salt and freshly ground black pepper to taste

6 ounces Gorgonzola cheese, crumbled

3/4 cup pine nuts, lightly toasted

In a small bowl, combine the raisins and wine.
Cover and let stand 2 hours to plump the raisins.
Drain and discard the liquid.

Place the lettuce in a large bowl. In a small bowl,
whisk together the olive oil and vinegar. Season with
salt and pepper. Pour the dressing over the lettuce
and toss to coat. Divide the lettuce onto 6 plates.
Top with the raisins, Gorgonzola, and pine nuts.

Serves 6
Serve with Ferrari-Carano Winery
Fumé Blanc Reserve

FETZER VINEYARDS

"Live right, Eat right, Pick the right grapes"™ sig-
nifies the Fetzer Vineyards philosophy toward wine
production and living in general. Fetzer has dedi-
cated itself to being an environmentally and socially
conscious grower, producer, and marketer of wines
of the highest quality and, to that end, farms 360
acres of certified organic grapes. Their award-
winning wines run the gamut from Johannisberg
Riesling to Reserve Cabernet Sauvignon. Based in
Mendocino County, Fetzer is one of the north
coast's finest producers of premium wine.

CUCUMBER-YOGURT SALAD
with Toy Box Tomatoes

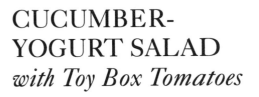

Toy box tomatoes are baby red and yellow tomatoes that may be found in specialty produce markets. Regular cherry tomatoes may be substituted in this delicious salad from John Ash's wonderful book **Earth to the Table: John Ash's Wine Country Cuisine.**

2 large English cucumbers

Kosher salt

1$\frac{1}{4}$ cups plain yogurt

1 cup minced red onions

1 tablespoon chopped fresh basil

1 tablespoon chopped fresh mint

2 teaspoons sugar

1 teaspoon minced garlic

$\frac{1}{2}$ teaspoon seeded and minced serrano chiles

$\frac{1}{2}$ teaspoon toasted and crushed cumin seed

$\frac{1}{4}$ teaspoon freshly ground black pepper

3 tablespoons seasoned rice vinegar

$\frac{1}{4}$ cup pine nuts, toasted

1 pint toy box tomatoes or cherry tomatoes

(recipe continued on next page)

With a vegetable peeler, remove the skin from the cucumbers in alternating strips. Cut the cucumbers in half lengthwise and scrape out the seeds with a teaspoon. Slice into 1/4-inch slices. Place in a colander in the sink. Lightly sprinkle the cucumber slices with kosher salt, toss, and set aside to drain for at least 1 hour.

In a large bowl, combine the yogurt, onions, basil, mint, sugar, garlic, chiles, cumin, and pepper.

Using a paper towel, blot the cucumber slices dry. Toss the cucumbers with the rice vinegar and add them to the yogurt-onion mixture. Cover and refrigerate at least 2 hours before serving. At serving time, stir in the pine nuts and the tomatoes.

Serves 6 to 8
Serve with Fetzer Vineyards
Gewürztraminer

1993

MENDOCINO
PETITE SIRAH
Upton Vineyards

GRAPES GROWN ORGANICALLY
CONTAINS NO DETECTABLE SULFITES
NO SULFITES ADDED
ALCOHOL 13.0% BY VOLUME

FREY VINEYARDS

A member of California Certified Organic Farmers, Frey Vineyards was one of the first to farm their vineyards organically and offer a wine from certified organically grown grapes. Located near the northernmost origins of the Russian River watershed, this Mendocino-appellation winery produces elegant, well-structured wines from its dry-farmed vineyards.

TOMATO TART
with Gruyère & Tarragon

Seductive aromas will arise to greet your guests when you slice into this beautiful tart.

2 tablespoons minced fresh tarragon

2 cloves garlic, minced

1 teaspoon Frey Vineyards Petite Syrah

5 tomatoes, peeled and thickly sliced

14 sheets phyllo dough

1/4 cup melted butter

1 1/2 tablespoons Dijon mustard

1 cup grated Gruyère cheese

Salt and freshly ground black pepper to taste

Preheat oven to 375 degrees F. Butter a 10-inch pie plate.

In a small bowl, combine the tarragon, garlic, and wine. Place the tomato slices in a shallow dish and spread with the tarragon mixture. Set aside.

Unfold the phyllo sheets. Use only one sheet at a time and keep the remaining sheets covered with a damp tea towel to keep them from drying out. Place one sheet of phyllo into the prepared pie plate. Using a pastry brush, lightly brush the phyllo with melted butter. Lay a second sheet on top of the first and brush with butter. Continue until all of the phyllo and melted butter is used. Trim the excess phyllo from around the pie plate. Spread the mustard in the bottom of the tart. Sprinkle evenly with the Gruyère. Arrange the tomatoes and the tarragon mixture on top. Season with salt and pepper. Bake for 30 minutes, or until lightly browned and the cheese is bubbly. Serve immediately.

Serves 6
Serve with Frey Vineyards
Petite Syrah

MERLOT
SONOMA COUNTY

GEYSER PEAK WINERY

Located just north of Healdsburg, 100-year-old Geyser Peak Winery's tradition of excellence shows in their being named "1998 Winery of the Year" by Wine & Spirits *magazine and the San Francisco International Wine Competition. Their original vine-covered stone winery is now the cornerstone of a state-of-the-art complex that is one of the most well equipped wineries in California. Within the winery, president and head winemaker Daryl Groom oversees the vinification of not only their sought-after reserve wines but also a multitude of great wines for all occasions.*

ROASTED EGGPLANT
Layered with Herbed Ricotta & Spicy Tomato Glaze

Serve this satisfying dish as a main course with a country salad.

2 eggplants
Olive oil

HERBED RICOTTA FILLING:

15 ounces ricotta cheese

4 ounces mozzarella cheese, grated

1/4 cup freshly grated Parmesan cheese

3 egg yolks

1 tablespoon minced parsley

1 green onion, minced

1 clove garlic, minced

1/2 teaspoon each salt freshly ground black pepper

SPICY TOMATO GLAZE:

1 tablespoon olive oil

1 clove garlic

1 can (15-ounces) tomato sauce

1 teaspoon oregano

1/2 teaspoon hot red chile flakes

2 ounces mozzarella cheese, grated

(recipe continued on next page)

🍂 Preheat oven to 450 degrees F. Lightly oil a baking sheet.

Trim off the top and bottom of the eggplants and discard. Slice the eggplants crosswise into 1/4-inch slices. Brush with olive oil and place on the prepared baking sheet. Roast for about 20 minutes, or until well browned and tender.

For the filling: In a bowl, stir together the ricotta, half of the mozzarella, the Parmesan, egg yolks, parsley, green onion, garlic, salt, and pepper until well blended.

For the glaze: In a saucepan, heat the oil over medium heat. Add the garlic and sauté until fragrant. Add the tomato sauce, oregano, and chile flakes. Bring to a simmer, reduce heat to medium-low, and cook until slightly thickened, about 15 minutes.

Reduce oven temperature to 350 degrees F. Lightly oil a 2 1/2-quart baking dish.

Layer half of the eggplant slices in the bottom of the baking dish, overlapping slices to cover the bottom completely. Spread filling evenly over the eggplant. Cover the filling with remaining eggplant slices. Spread glaze evenly over the top. Sprinkle with remaining mozzarella. Bake for 35 to 40 minutes, or until heated through and bubbly.

Serves 6
Serve with Geyser Peak
Merlot

GLORIA FERRER
CHAMPAGNE CAVES

Founded by José Ferrer, son of Pedro Ferrer Bosch, the Spanish-Catalan founder of Freixenet, Gloria Ferrer Champagne Caves was opened to the public in July of 1986. Named for José Ferrer's beloved wife, Gloria, the winery has been winning awards and the accolades of wine critics ever since. Located within the cool Carneros appellation, the beautiful building with stucco walls, arched windows, and overhanging balconies is a piece of the proud history of old Spain.

POTATO
CROQUETTES

There is something intriguingly romantic about croquettes. These are sublimely delicious.

1 pound potatoes, peeled and cut into 2-inch cubes

1/4 cup freshly grated Parmesan cheese

1 egg, lightly beaten

2 tablespoons minced onion

1 tablespoon minced fresh Italian parsley

1 clove garlic, minced

Salt and freshly ground black pepper to taste

2 cups fresh bread crumbs, divided

Olive oil for frying

In a pot, combine the potatoes with salted water to cover. Bring to a boil and cook until the potatoes are very tender. Drain and mash until smooth. Set aside to cool.

In a large bowl, whisk together the Parmesan, egg, onion, parsley, garlic, salt, and pepper. Add the mashed potatoes and stir until just combined. Add 1 cup of the bread crumbs and stir until just blended. Form into walnut-sized balls and roll in the remaining bread crumbs. In a large skillet, heat 1/8-inch of olive oil over medium-high heat. Add the croquettes, reduce heat to medium, and fry until golden brown on all sides. Serve immediately.

Serves 4 to 6
Serve with Gloria Ferrer Champagne Caves
Sonoma Brut

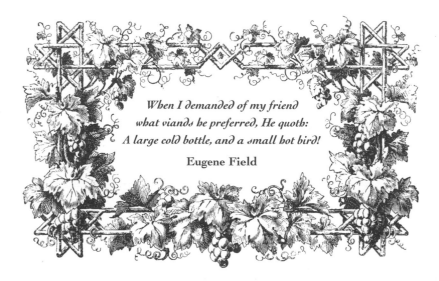

When I demanded of my friend
what viands he preferred, He quoth:
A large cold bottle, and a small hot bird!

Eugene Field

GLEN ELLEN WINERY

Glen Ellen Winery was created in 1983 by the Benziger family with the idea of producing inexpensive and delicious varietal wines to an increasing number of wine consumers. Thus was born the whole category of "fighting varietals." The winery is situated in Sonoma, California, with a wonderful visitors' center located in the charming town of Glen Ellen in the historic Valley of the Moon. In 1994, the Benzigers sold the winery to United Distillers and Vintners. UDV continues to produce Glen Ellen Proprietors Reserve wines with the same degree of dedication to quality—not surprising, as the winemaking team has virtually remained the same for nearly a decade. Glen Ellen utilizes an innovative program, the Grower Feedback Loop, to encourage their many growers to improve the quality of the fruit produced each year to meet the growing sophistication of consumers.

CARAMELIZED ONION WAFFLES
with Creamed Spinach

Excite your guests with these supremely delicious dinner waffles.

CARAMELIZED ONIONS:

3 tablespoons butter

2 onions, finely chopped

1 tablespoon water

1/2 teaspoon salt

1/2 teaspoon sugar

CREAMED SPINACH:

2 tablespoons butter

1 pound fresh baby spinach, washed well
    and chopped

2 cloves garlic, minced

3/4 cup heavy cream

1/4 cup sour cream

1/8 teaspoon freshly grated nutmeg

Salt and freshly ground black pepper to taste

(recipe continued on next page)

WAFFLES:

$1^{1}/2$ cups all-purpose flour

2 tablespoons minced fresh Italian parsley

2 tablespoons minced fresh chives

1 tablespoon baking powder

1 teaspoon freshly ground black pepper

$1/2$ teaspoon salt

1 cup milk

$1/4$ cup melted butter

2 eggs

Melted butter for the waffle iron

For the onions: In a large skillet, melt the butter over medium heat. Add the onions and toss to coat. Add the water, salt, and sugar and toss to coat. Reduce heat to medium-low and cover skillet tightly. Simmer about 30 minutes, stirring often, until the onions are deep golden brown and very tender. Set aside to cool completely.

For the spinach: In a large skillet, melt the butter over medium heat. Add the spinach and sauté until wilted. Add the garlic and sauté until fragrant. Stir in the cream, sour cream, nutmeg, salt, and pepper. Simmer until thickened. Set aside and keep warm.

For the waffles: In a large bowl, stir together the flour, parsley, chives, baking powder, pepper, and salt until evenly blended. In a separate bowl, whisk together the milk, melted butter, and eggs until smooth. Stir milk mixture into flour mixture until just combined. Fold in the reserved caramelized onions. Do not overmix. The batter will be somewhat lumpy.

Preheat a waffle iron and brush with a little melted butter. Cook waffles 3 to 5 minutes, or until done. Keep waffles hot in a warm oven while cooking the remaining waffles. Brush the waffle iron with more melted butter between each waffle.

Place a waffle on each plate and top with the creamed spinach.

Serves 6
Serve with Glen Ellen Winery
Pinot Noir

**GROWN, PRODUCED AND BOTTLED BY THE H.A. OSWALD FAMILY
PHILO, CA. ALCOHOL 12.85% BY VOLUME, RESIDUAL SUGAR 0.8%**

HUSCH VINEYARDS

Husch Vineyards is a small family winery and the first bonded winery located in the Anderson Valley appellation of Mendocino County in northern California a picturesque 2^1/2-hours' drive north of San Francisco. All Husch wines are made from grapes grown in the family-owned vineyards. Some of the wines are distributed throughout the United States, but many are available only locally or at their tasting room. Quality is the key word at the winery. It shows in the care that goes into growing fine grapes in the attention given in each step of the winemaking process and in the time given to visitors who come to the winery for tastings.

HARVEST SQUASH SOUP
with Ancho Chile Cream

*The ancho chile gives this winter soup a touch
of heat that even non-chile lovers will adore.*

1 butternut squash, about 4 pounds, peeled and
    cut into 2-inch chunks

1 onion, chopped

1 clove garlic, chopped

1 bay leaf

2$\frac{1}{2}$ cups vegetable stock

1 cup Husch Vineyards Gewürztraminer

Salt and freshly ground black pepper to taste

1 dried ancho chile, stemmed and seeded

$\frac{1}{2}$ cup heavy cream

(recipe continued on next page)

In a pot, combine the squash, onion, garlic, bay leaf, stock, and wine and bring to a boil. Reduce heat to medium-low, cover, and simmer for 1 hour, or until the vegetables are very tender. Purée in batches in a blender. Return the soup to the pot, season with salt and pepper, and heat through.

In a small saucepan, combine the chile and cream and bring to a boil. Remove from heat, cover, and let stand for 30 minutes. Purée the chile and cream in a food processor until smooth.

To serve, ladle soup into bowls and top with a dollop of the chile cream.

Serves 6 to 8
Serve with Husch Vineyards
Gewürztraminer

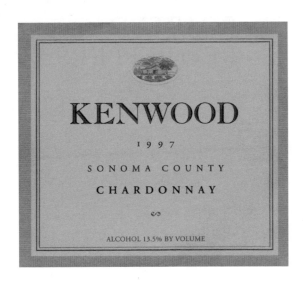

KENWOOD
1997
SONOMA COUNTY
CHARDONNAY

ALCOHOL 13.5% BY VOLUME

KENWOOD VINEYARDS
AND WINERY

At Kenwood Vineyards and Winery each vineyard lot is handled separately within the winery to preserve its individuality. Such "small lot" winemaking allows the winemaker to bring each lot of wine to its fullest potential. This style of winemaking is evident in the quality of Kenwood's special bottlings. From the Jack London Vineyard series, whose grapes come from the historical lava-terraced vineyards of the Jack London Ranch, to the Artist Series Cabernet Sauvignon, whose labels each year feature the work of a renowned artist, Kenwood shows Sonoma County at its best.

TEQUILA SHOOTER ROASTED RED PEPPERS

4 red bell peppers

2 tablespoons olive oil

Salt and freshly ground black pepper to taste

4 ounces Monterey jack cheese, grated

$1/2$ cup chopped fresh cilantro

1 serrano chile, minced

2 cloves garlic, minced

1 tablespoon tequila

1 teaspoon freshly squeezed lime juice

Preheat oven to 400 degrees F. Lightly oil a baking dish.

Cut the tops off the bell peppers and remove the seeds and veins. Brush the peppers with olive oil and season with salt and pepper. Roast in the oven until the skin is slightly blackened and the peppers still hold their shape. Remove

from the oven and place in a plastic bag to steam.
When cool, remove and discard the skin.

Reduce oven temperature to 350 degrees F.

In a bowl, stir together the cheese, cilantro,
chile, garlic, tequila, and lime juice until blended.
Divide the cheese mixture and stuff into the
roasted peppers. Lay the peppers on their sides in
the baking dish and season with salt and pepper.
Bake for 10 to 15 minutes, or until the cheese is
melted. Serve immediately.

Serves 4
Serve with Kenwood Vineyards and Winery
Chardonnay

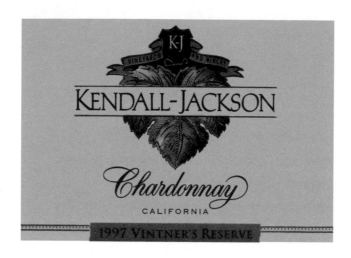

KENDALL-JACKSON WINERY

In 1974, Jess Jackson and his family purchased an 85-acre pear ranch near Lakeport in Northern California. By 1982, the ranch was a vineyard, the barn was a tasting room, and the pasture was a winery. Meanwhile, they studied the premium vineyards that span California's cool coastal growing regions and discovered the wonderful spectrum of flavors produced by the same grape varietal grown in different locations. Why not use this exciting diversity? Why not blend the best grapes from the best vineyards to produce unique wines with layers of depth and complexity? Their first Chardonnay was made in 1982, from vineyards in Santa Barbara, Monterey, Sonoma, and Lake Counties. This wine was named "Best American Chardonnay" by the American Wine Competition. Their concept of blending the best with the best was affirmed and to this day continues to be the reason their wines are noted for their consistency and complexity, vintage after vintage.

WARM POTATO TIMBALES *with Goat Cheese & Chanterelle Mushrooms*

Chefs Tess McDonough and Ed Walsh once again have shattered culinary barriers with these beguilingly rich timbales.

1 cup chanterelle mushrooms, sliced

$1/2$ cup olive oil

Salt and freshly ground black pepper to taste

2 onions, finely chopped

2 tablespoons water

1 bunch Swiss chard, finely chopped

1 pound yellow Finn potatoes, peeled and cut into 1-inch cubes

6 ounces goat cheese, crumbled

1 teaspoon minced fresh oregano

1 teaspoon minced fresh parsley

1 teaspoon minced fresh thyme

4 cups mixed baby greens

1 tablespoon balsamic vinegar

(recipe continued on next page)

Preheat oven to 375 degrees F. Lightly oil a baking sheet.

Place the mushrooms on the prepared baking sheet. Brush with 2 tablespoons of the olive oil and season with salt and pepper. Bake for 15 minutes. Remove from the oven and set aside. Reduce oven temperature to 300 degrees F.

In a skillet, heat 3 tablespoons of the olive oil over medium heat. Add the onions and sauté until tender. Reduce the heat to low and add the water. Cover the skillet and cook until the onions are a deep golden brown. Stir occasionally and check to see if the mixture needs more water to prevent scorching. Transfer the onions to a large bowl.

In the same skillet, heat 3 tablespoons of the olive oil over medium heat. Add the Swiss chard and sauté until tender. Transfer the Swiss chard to the bowl with the onions.

Bring a pot of salted water to a boil. Add the potatoes and cook until tender but not mushy. Drain the potatoes and transfer them to the onion mixture. Toss the vegetables together and season with salt and pepper. Set aside.

In a small bowl, stir together the goat cheese, oregano, parsley, and thyme until smooth. Set aside.

In a bowl, toss the baby greens with the remaining olive oil and the balsamic vinegar. Set aside.

Lightly oil a baking sheet and 4 individual 3-inch ring molds.

To assemble the timbales: Place the ring molds on the prepared baking sheet. Divide the potato mixture and firmly pack into the molds, leaving 1/4-inch headspace from the top. Fill the rest of the mold with the goat cheese mixture. Bake for 10 to 15 minutes, or until the top is lightly browned. Remove from oven and let rest for 2 minutes.

Divide the greens onto 4 plates. Run a small sharp knife around the inside of the molds to loosen. Carefully lift off the molds. With a spatula, carefully slide the timbales onto the greens. Sprinkle the chanterelles on top and serve immediately.

Serves 4
Serve with Kendall-Jackson Winery
Chardonnay

KORBEL CHAMPAGNE CELLARS

Located just east of Guerneville and just a handful of miles inland from the Pacific Ocean, Korbel Champagne Cellars is a name that has stood for fine méthode-champenoise sparkling wines for over a hundred years. Founded in the late 1880s by three immigrant brothers from Bohemia—Francis, Anton, and Joseph Korbel—and owned and managed by the Heck family since 1954, Korbel has developed into one of California's most respected champagne houses.

ASPARAGUS
& Sautéed Vegetable Salad

Begin your meal with this delicious warm salad from chef Curtis Aikens. It combines fresh vegetables and savory spices for a hearty first course.

¹/4 cup olive oil

3 garlic cloves, minced

1 tablespoon grated fresh ginger

¹/2 red bell pepper, diced

¹/2 yellow bell pepper, diced

8 ounces tofu, cut into ¹/2-inch cubes

8 ounces eggplant, cut into ¹/2-inch cubes

¹/4 cup Korbel Chardonnay Champagne

¹/4 cup vegetable stock

8 ounces asparagus, cut into 1-inch pieces
and steamed until tender

2 tablespoons minced fresh parsley

1 head of iceberg lettuce, shredded

(recipe continued on next page)

In a saucepan, heat 2 tablespoons of the oil over medium heat. Add the garlic, ginger, bell peppers, and tofu. Cover and simmer 4 minutes. Add the remaining oil and the eggplant. Simmer, uncovered, an additional 3 minutes. Add the Korbel Chardonnay Champagne and stock. Stir with a wooden spoon until the liquid is reduced, about 3 to 5 minutes. Stir in the asparagus and parsley. Arrange the lettuce on a large platter. Spoon the warm vegetables over and serve immediately.

Serves 6
Serve with Korbel
Chardonnay Champagne

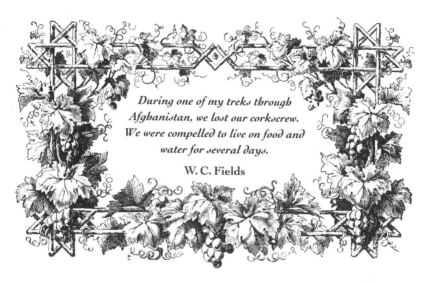

During one of my treks through Afghanistan, we lost our corkscrew. We were compelled to live on food and water for several days.

W. C. Fields

LA CREMA

La Crema has focused its efforts on the viticultural areas within the cool Carneros and Russian River appellations as well as in the yet "undiscovered" regions that lie alongside those two winegrowing areas. The influence of cool maritime climates, coupled with painstaking attention given to each individual lot of wine, has helped develop La Crema into one of Sonoma County's leading wineries.

SUMMER
SPINACH SALAD
with Jarlsberg Croutons

Serve this satisfying salad during the dog days of summer.

1 tablespoon honey

1 tablespoon mirin

1 tablespoon grainy mustard

1 tablespoon rice vinegar

Salt and freshly ground black pepper to taste

1/2 cup olive oil

1 bunch radishes, thinly sliced

1 red onion, thinly sliced

1 cup fresh corn kernels

1 cup thinly sliced fresh mushrooms

8 ounces fresh baby spinach

4 ounces Jarlsberg cheese, grated

8 slices sourdough baguette

In a bowl, whisk together the honey, mirin, mustard, vinegar, salt, and pepper. Whisk in the olive oil. Add the radishes, red onion, corn, and mushrooms and toss to coat. Divide the spinach onto 4 plates and spoon the vegetables and dressing on top.

Preheat the broiler. Divide the cheese onto the baguette slices and broil until bubbly. Place the croutons on the salads and serve immediately.

Serves 4
Serve with La Crema Winery
Chardonnay

LEDSON VINEYARDS
AND WINERY

One of Northern California's newest wineries, Ledson is rapidly making a name for itself with its reserve Merlots, floral and fruity Rieslings, and intense Chardonnays. Located in Sonoma County's Valley of the Moon, Ledson is at home in a fantastic brick-and-mortar Gothic-style mansion known affectionately as "The Castle." Two full-time chefs guarantee Ledson's commitment to the art and culture of pairing food and great wine.

MOZZARELLA MARINARA

This sublime marinara sauce is the secret behind these perennial favorites.

MARINARA SAUCE:

3 tablespoons olive oil

1 onion, chopped

1 carrot, chopped

1/2 cup chopped green bell pepper

4 cloves garlic, minced

1/2 cup Ledson Vineyards and Winery Merlot

1 can (28-ounces) tomatoes and their juice

1 tablespoon tomato paste

1 teaspoon salt

1 teaspoon oregano

1/2 teaspoon basil

1/2 teaspoon thyme

1/2 teaspoon freshly ground black pepper

1/4 teaspoon hot red chile flakes

(recipe continued on next page)

1 pound mozzarella cheese

3 eggs, lightly beaten

1 tablespoon water

1 cup all-purpose flour

2 cups Italian-seasoned bread crumbs

1/3 cup olive oil

Chopped fresh Italian parsley

🍃 **For the sauce:** In a large saucepan, heat the olive oil over medium heat. Add the onion, carrot, green bell pepper, and garlic and sauté until tender. Stir in the wine and bring to a simmer. Add the tomatoes, tomato paste, salt, oregano, basil, thyme, pepper, and red chile flakes and bring to a simmer. Cover the saucepan, reduce heat to medium-low, and continue to simmer for about 1 1/2 hours, or until the flavors marry and the sauce is thick. In a blender, pureé in batches until smooth. Return the marinara sauce to the saucepan and keep warm.

Cut the cheese into 6 equal rectangles, approximately 4 inches long and 1 inch wide. In a shallow bowl, whisk together the eggs and water until smooth. Place the flour in a separate shallow bowl and the bread crumbs in a third shallow bowl. Coat the cheese with flour and shake off the excess. Dip the cheese in the egg mixture, then dredge in the bread crumbs, coating completely. Arrange the coated cheese pieces on a plate without touching each other. Cover loosely with plastic wrap and chill 1 hour.

In a large nonstick skillet, heat the $1/3$ cup of olive oil over medium-high heat. When the oil is hot, add the cheese and cook until golden brown on all sides. Ladle the marinara sauce onto 6 plates and top with a piece of mozzarella. Sprinkle with parsley and serve immediately.

Serves 6
Serve with Ledson Vineyards and Winery Merlot

LOUIS MARTINI

Louis Martini wines are made in the classic tradition, to accompany food, to enhance its flavor, and to celebrate the sharing of mealtime among family and friends. The Martinis have always made wines that they drink themselves, in the belief that others will take pleasure in them as well. They say their wines are not made to win awards, although they win acclaim time and time again. They say their wines are not made to be museum pieces, although they have made history with their pioneering winemaking techniques. They say their wines are made simply to enjoy. Since they first settled in the Napa Valley over 60 years ago, the Martinis have been part of the history of Northern California winemaking, and their commitment to the vine is evident to all who visit the winery or taste their wines.

FETTUCCINE *with* Roasted Red Pepper Sauce

When the urge for pasta strikes, try this excellent version from Louis Martini.

2 red bell peppers

1 tablespoon olive oil

1/2 cup freshly grated Parmesan cheese

1/2 cup ricotta cheese

2 cloves garlic, minced

1/4 teaspoon hot red chile flakes

1 pound fresh fettuccine

2 tablespoons butter

Salt and freshly ground black pepper to taste

1 tablespoon minced fresh parsley

Preheat oven to 450 degrees F. Lightly oil a baking sheet.

Brush the bell peppers with the olive oil and place on the prepared baking sheet. Roast the peppers for about 30 minutes or until blackened. Remove from oven and place the hot peppers in a plastic bag. Let them steam in the bag until cool. Remove the skins and discard.

(recipe continued on next page)

Place the peeled peppers in the bowl of a food processor and pulse until smooth. Add the Parmesan, ricotta, garlic, and red chile flakes and process until smooth.

Cook the fettuccine in boiling salted water until al dente, then drain. Return the drained pasta to the pot and toss with the butter. Gently stir in the sauce until evenly coated. Season with salt and pepper. Divide onto 4 plates and sprinkle with parsley.

Serves 4
Serve with Louis Martini
Merlot

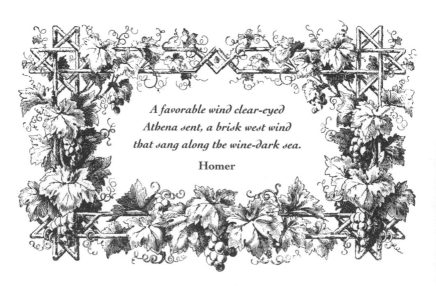

A favorable wind clear-eyed
Athena sent, a brisk west wind
that sang along the wine-dark sea.

Homer

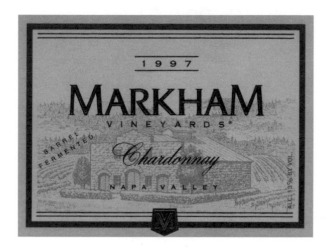

MARKHAM
VINEYARDS

Markham Vineyards has, for over twenty years, rewarded eonophiles with wines of a consistency and level of quality seldom matched in the Napa Valley. From its historic stone winery, built in 1873 by Jean Laurent, an immigrant from Bordeaux, Markham crafts outstanding wines that are unpretentious in style and are meant to be enjoyed. Vineyards from San Pablo Bay north to Calistoga provide a wealth of different growing conditions for both their white and red wines.

FOUR CHEESE TART

Linda Thomas, from Linda Thomas Catering Company, created this rich and savory tart, which would be lovely served with fresh figs or pears.

4 ounces Gruyère, grated

2 ounces soft goat cheese, crumbled

2 ounces Gorgonzola, crumbled

1/8 teaspoon freshly grated nutmeg

2 tablespoons butter

2 tablespoons all-purpose flour

1/2 cup half-and-half

3 ounces Brie, rind trimmed off

1 pre-baked 9-inch pastry shell

1/4 cup snipped fresh chives

🍇 Preheat oven to 350 degrees F.

In a bowl, stir together the Gruyère, goat cheese, Gorgonzola, and nutmeg. Set aside.

In a saucepan, melt the butter over medium heat. Whisk in the flour until smooth. Continue to cook, whisking constantly, for 2 minutes. Slowly pour in the half-and-half, whisking constantly, until smooth. Continue to cook, whisking constantly, until the mixture is thick. Stir in the Brie until melted. Pour the mixture into the reserved bowl of cheeses and stir until blended. Spread the cheese mixture evenly into the pastry shell. Bake for 10 to 15 minutes, or until the top turns a light golden brown. Remove from oven and allow to cool before serving. Sprinkle with chives and cut into thin wedges.

Serves 8
Serve with Markham Vineyards
Chardonnay

MUMM CUVÉE NAPA

Journey through the vineyards, along the peaceful Silverado Trail, to the glorious home of Mumm Cuvée Napa. Imagine yourself on a terrace, seated under the cool shade of an elegant umbrella. The sun is setting over the Mayacamas Mountains in the distance, with soft amber and purple hues settling over the hills and vineyards. These images are reflected in your hand by a flute of America's finest sparkling wine—Mumm Cuvée Napa.

STUFFED PUMPKIN BLOSSOMS
with Tomato Coulis

If necessary, you can substitute squash blossoms for this impossibly romantic main course.

TOMATO COULIS:

1 tablespoon butter

1 tablespoon minced shallot

1 clove garlic, minced

6 Roma tomatoes, peeled, seeded, and chopped

Salt and freshly ground black pepper to taste

$^1/_2$ cup ricotta cheese

3 eggs

2 tablespoons grated fontina cheese

1 tablespoon minced fresh parsley

$^1/_8$ teaspoon freshly grated nutmeg

Salt and freshly ground black pepper to taste

12 large pumpkin blossoms

2 tablespoons butter

1 tablespoon olive oil

(recipe continued on next page)

🍃 **For the tomato coulis:** In a saucepan, melt the butter over medium heat. Add the shallot and garlic and sauté until tender. Add the tomatoes and simmer until tender. Remove from heat and set aside.

In a bowl, whisk together the ricotta, 1 of the eggs, fontina, parsley, nutmeg, salt, and pepper until blended. Carefully place 1 tablespoon of the mixture into each pumpkin blossom. Lightly twist the tips of the blossom to seal. Continue until all blossoms and filling are used.

Place the remaining 2 eggs in a small shallow dish and beat until smooth. In a large skillet, heat the butter and olive oil together over medium heat. Dip the filled blossoms in the beaten eggs and let the excess drain off. Place the blossoms in the hot skillet and cook until golden brown on both sides.

Divide the tomato coulis onto 4 plates. Place the pumpkin blossoms on top of the tomato coulis and serve immediately.

Serves 4
Serve with Mumm Cuvée Napa
Brut Prestige

MINER FAMILY VINEYARDS
AND WINERY

Located on the Silverado Trail in a new and modern winery, Miner Family Vineyards and Winery produces inky dark Cabernets and Merlots as well as complex and balanced Chardonnays from their estate vineyards high up in the eastern hills of the Oakville appellation of the Napa Valley. Low yields from the ancient, rocky volcanic soil serve to amplify and intensify the structure of these classic Napa Valley wines. Additionally, small lots of Sauvignon Blanc, Viognier, Pinot Noir, Zinfandel, Syrah, and Sangiovese are available in limited quantities.

STUFFED
ZUCCHINI

Susan Bishop brought the flavors of Italy alive in this tasty main course.

6 baby zucchini, each about 6 inches long

Salt and freshly ground black pepper to taste

3 tablespoons olive oil

1 onion, finely chopped

3 cloves garlic, minced

1 bunch Swiss chard, finely chopped and steamed
   until tender

1/2 cup finely chopped fresh basil

1 teaspoon minced fresh oregano

1 teaspoon minced fresh rosemary

1 teaspoon minced fresh sage

1 cup ricotta cheese

1 egg, lightly beaten

1/2 cup fresh sourdough bread crumbs

1 cup grated Asiago cheese

Preheat oven to 375 degrees F. Lightly oil a
9 x 9-inch baking dish.

Place the whole zucchini in a steamer and steam
until barely tender. Remove and let cool. Cut in

half lengthwise and, with a teaspoon, scoop out the flesh taking care not to tear the shell. Chop the zucchini flesh, place it in a strainer or colander, and squeeze out as much liquid as possible. Transfer the zucchini flesh to a bowl. Sprinkle the insides of the zucchini shells with salt and pepper and set aside.

In a skillet, heat the olive oil over medium heat. Add the onion and garlic and sauté until tender. Transfer the onion mixture to the bowl of zucchini flesh. Add the Swiss chard, basil, oregano, rosemary, and sage and stir to mix. In a small bowl, whisk together the ricotta and egg, then stir into the vegetable mixture. Stir in the bread crumbs, making sure they are evenly distributed. Season with salt and pepper.

Place the reserved zucchini shells, cut side up, in the prepared baking dish. Mound the vegetable mixture inside the zucchini shells. Sprinkle with Asiago cheese. Bake for 30 minutes, or until the cheese is melted and the tops are golden brown. Serve immediately.

Serves 6
Serve with Miner Family Vineyards and Winery
Zinfandel

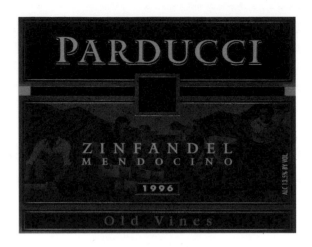

PARDUCCI
WINE ESTATES

There are only two things you need to know about a wine. First, do you like it? Second, can you afford it? The people at Parducci are confident that, after tasting and pricing Parducci wines, the answer to both questions will be an emphatic "Yes!" They have always recognized that wine customers enjoy a variety of wines. As such, they have taken advantage of the numerous varieties grown in Mendocino County and now produce all the following: Cabernet Sauvignon, Chenin Blanc, Pinot Noir, Chardonnay, Charbono, Barbera, Petite Sirah, Merlot, Sauvignon Blanc, Zinfandel, Syrah, and Sangiovese. Parducci strives to bring out the varietal characteristics each grape has to offer, and believes that wine is an honest, natural product that should never be over-processed. It should have a softness that invites pleasant consumption upon release.

GORGONZOLA STRATA

Strata is a combination of comfort food and elegant high cuisine. It never fails to delight hungry guests.

12 ounces Gorgonzola cheese, crumbled

12 ounces cream cheese, softened and cut into small pieces

2^1/2 cups milk

5 eggs

2 teaspoons minced fresh rosemary

^{1}/2 teaspoon salt

^{1}/2 teaspoon white pepper

^{1}/4 teaspoon Tabasco sauce

1 loaf (16-ounces) challah bread, cut into 2-inch cubes and toasted

Preheat oven to 325 degrees F. Lightly butter a 2-quart baking dish.

In a large bowl, combine the Gorgonzola, cream cheese, milk, eggs, rosemary, salt, white pepper, and Tabasco sauce. With a mixer, beat on low speed until the mixture is somewhat smooth.

Place the toasted challah into the prepared baking dish and pour the egg mixture over. Allow to stand for 30 minutes. Bake for about 50 minutes or until the custard is set. Serve immediately.

Serves 6 to 8
Serve with Parducci Wine Estates
Zinfandel

PEJU PROVINCE

Peju Province is one of the few family-owned and operated wineries in the Napa Valley. The winery's thirty acres of quality vineyards are located in the famed Rutherford bench, Napa's renowned Cabernet region. In addition to Cabernet Sauvignon, Chardonnay, Merlot, and Cabernet Franc, Peju Province produces small lots of unusual wines such as their Carnival, Provence, and Late Harvest. The winery's long-term commitment to quality has won accolades from many in the wine trade, and their wines are sought after by a growing cadre of wine lovers and aficionados.

STIR-FRIED GREEN TOMATOES

Herta Peju discovered a version of this recipe on a recent visit to the southern part of the United States.

1 tablespoon olive oil

1 cup chopped green bell pepper

1 cup chopped red bell pepper

1 onion, chopped

1 Anaheim chile, seeded and diced

1/2 teaspoon freshly grated nutmeg

2 ripe tomatoes, quartered

3 green tomatoes, sliced

Salt and freshly ground black pepper to taste

In a large skillet, heat the olive oil over medium heat. Add the bell peppers, onion, and Anaheim chile and stir-fry until tender. Add the nutmeg and stir-fry until fragrant. Add the ripe tomatoes and stir-fry until just tender. Add the green tomatoes and stir-fry until tender. Season with salt and pepper. Serve immediately.

Serves 4
Serve with Peju Province Winery
Chardonnay

UNFILTERED

1996

ROBERT MONDAVI

NAPA VALLEY

PINOT NOIR

ROBERT MONDAVI
WINERY

Founded in 1966 by Robert Mondavi and his son, Michael, the Robert Mondavi Winery is considered a leader in the modern wine industry. They are committed to producing naturally balanced wines of great finesse and elegance that complement and enhance fine food. They have been successful in achieving these goals through earth-friendly farming practices, a sophisticated winery emphasizing gentle treatment of their wines, and a genuine love for their handiwork. No other winery epitomizes the Napa Valley quite like the Robert Mondavi Winery.

EGGPLANT TIMBALES *with Tomato Sauce & Gorgonzola Sauce*

This imaginative first course from caterer Patricia Caringella traces its roots back to her Italian past.

EGGPLANT TIMBALES:

5 tablespoons olive oil

1 medium eggplant, peeled and cut into 1/4-inch cubes

2 cloves garlic, minced

1 cup heavy cream

3/4 cup freshly grated Parmesan cheese

1 egg

Salt and freshly ground black pepper to taste

TOMATO SAUCE:

1/4 cup olive oil

1 clove garlic, minced

8 Roma tomatoes, peeled, seeded, and chopped

1/2 cup Robert Mondavi Pinot Noir

Salt and freshly ground black pepper to taste

1 tablespoon minced fresh basil

1 tablespoon minced fresh Italian parsley

(recipe continued on next page)

GORGONZOLA SAUCE:

1/2 cup heavy cream

2 ounces Gorgonzola cheese, crumbled

1 tablespoon butter

1 tablespoon sour cream

Salt and freshly ground black pepper to taste

🍃 Preheat oven to 375 degrees F. Butter 4 individual 3/4-cup molds.

For the eggplant timbales: In a large skillet, heat the olive oil over medium heat. Add the eggplant and sauté until golden brown, about 20 to 25 minutes. Add the garlic and sauté until fragrant. Add the cream and cook until the cream is absorbed. Transfer the mixture into the bowl of a food processor and process until smooth. Add the Parmesan and egg and process until smooth. Season with salt and pepper. Divide the mixture into the prepared molds and place in a large pan. Add enough water to come half way up the sides of the molds. Bake for 20 minutes or until firm.

For the tomato sauce: In a large skillet, heat the olive oil over medium heat. Add the garlic and sauté until fragrant. Add the tomatoes and wine. Bring to a boil, then reduce heat to medium-low and simmer until thick. Season with salt and pepper. Stir in basil and parsley and remove from heat.

For the Gorgonzola sauce: In a small saucepan, combine the cream, Gorgonzola, butter, and sour cream. Whisk over low heat until smooth. Season with salt and pepper.

To serve, divide the tomato sauce onto 4 plates. Unmold the timbales onto the tomato sauce. Spoon the Gorgonzola sauce on top of each timbale.

Serves 4
Serve with Robert Mondavi Winery
Pinot Noir

*O thou the drink of gods,
and angels! Wine!*

Robert Herrick

RODNEY STRONG
VINEYARDS

Over 35 years ago Rodney Strong was one of the first to recognize Sonoma County's potential for excellence. After searching for vineyard land that would bring each grape variety to its fullest potential, Rodney Strong finally selected vineyard sites in the Chalk Hill, Alexander Valley, and Russian River Valley appellations to produce his wine. In the cellar, he employs the subtle use of barrel and stainless steel fermentation, oak aging, and other winemaking techniques to bring out the best in the fruit. All this is in keeping with his philosophy to allow the grapes from each vineyard to express their individual character in the final bottled wine.

BLACK BEAN SOUP

*On a cold winter day nothing warms better
than this thick and hearty soup.*

1 pound dried black beans

3 tablespoons olive oil

2 onions, chopped

2 carrots, chopped

1 rib celery, chopped

4 cloves garlic, minced

2 teaspoons cumin

1 teaspoon chili powder

$1/2$ teaspoon cayenne

$1/2$ teaspoon freshly ground black pepper

1 cup Rodney Strong Vineyards Pinot Noir

5 cups vegetable stock

$1/3$ cup chopped cilantro

1 teaspoon salt

Sour cream

(recipe continued on next page)

 Rinse the beans in cold water. Place the beans in a bowl and cover with plenty of cold water. Let stand overnight. The next day, drain the beans in a colander and set aside.

In a large pot, heat the olive oil over medium heat. Add the onions, carrots, celery, and garlic and sauté until tender. Stir in the cumin, chili powder, cayenne, and pepper and sauté until fragrant. Stir in the wine and bring to a simmer. Stir in the vegetable stock and reserved beans and bring to a simmer. Reduce heat to medium-low, cover the pot, and simmer for about 1 hour, or until the beans are tender. Remove the lid and stir in the cilantro and salt. Simmer until the soup is thick. Place half of the soup in a blender and purée until smooth. Return the soup to the pot and heat through. Serve in bowls with a dollop of sour cream.

Serves 6 to 8
Serve with Rodney Strong Vineyards
Pinot Noir

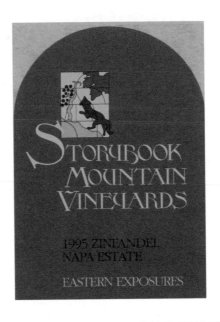

STORYBOOK MOUNTAIN VINEYARDS

At the extreme northern end of the Napa Valley lies Storybook Mountain Vineyards. Storybook Mountain is totally dedicated to Zinfandel and has established a worldwide reputation for consistently high quality. Proprietors Jerry and Sigrid Seps age their Zinfandel a minimum of 12 months inside century-old caves dug deep into the volcanic rock underlying their vineyards. Their wines are famed for their elegance and longevity. Notes of raspberries, black cherries, and spices are the keynotes of these complex, well-balanced wines.

ZINFANDEL
RISOTTO

*This dish highlights and mirrors the complex
flavors of the Storybook Mountain Zinfandel.*

1/4 cup olive oil

1 onion, finely chopped

2 cloves garlic, minced

1 teaspoon minced fresh sage

1/2 teaspoon minced fresh rosemary

2 cups Arborio rice

1 1/2 cups Storybook Mountain Eastern Exposures
Zinfandel

4 cups water

1/2 cup freshly grated Parmesan cheese

2 tablespoons butter

🍇 In a large saucepan, heat the olive oil over medium heat. Add the onion and garlic and sauté until tender. Stir in the sage and rosemary and sauté until fragrant. Add the rice and toss to coat. Lower the heat under the rice to medium-low.

In a separate saucepan, bring the wine to a simmer over medium-low heat. Pour the simmering wine into the rice and stir constantly until the rice has absorbed almost all of the liquid. In a separate saucepan, bring the water to a simmer over medium-low heat. Ladle enough simmering water into the rice to just cover, and stir until the rice has absorbed almost all of the liquid. Repeat this process until the rice is tender but still firm. This will take about 20 minutes. Stir in the Parmesan and butter until smooth. Serve immediately.

Serves 4 to 6
Serve with Storybook Mountain Eastern Exposures Zinfandel

STERLING VINEYARDS

Built in the architectural style of the Greek island of Mykonos, the Sterling Vineyards winery sits dramatically atop a 300-foot knoll just south of Napa Valley's northernmost town, Calistoga. Its white, monastic buildings contrast sharply with the dark green trees that cover the knoll. Visitors are carried up to the winery by aerial tramway and treated to a spectacular view of the Napa Valley below, as well as a close-up look at the Napa Valley's most dramatic and recognizable winery. The panorama is awe-inspiring and peaceful, punctuated only by the peal of Sterling's antique English church bells.

HERBED POLENTA
with Fontina Sauce
& Mushroom Ragù

*The subtle flavors of polenta shine under
the rich fontina sauce and mushrooms.*

HERBED POLENTA:

4 cups water

1/2 teaspoon salt

1 cup coarse cornmeal

1/2 teaspoon minced fresh rosemary

1/2 teaspoon minced fresh sage

1/2 teaspoon minced fresh thyme

MUSHROOM RAGÙ:

3 tablespoons olive oil

2 cloves garlic, minced

1 pound mushrooms, sliced

Salt and freshly ground black pepper to taste

(recipe continued on next page)

FONTINA SAUCE:

2 tablespoons butter

1 tablespoon flour

1 cup milk

8 ounces fontina cheese, grated

Salt and freshly ground black pepper to taste

3 tablespoons butter

1/4 cup minced fresh Italian parsley

Butter a 8 x 8-inch baking dish.

For the polenta: In a large saucepan, bring the water and salt to a boil. Reduce heat to medium and keep the water at a bare simmer. Slowly add the cornmeal in a thin stream, whisking constantly. Add the rosemary, sage, and thyme and continue to stir vigorously with a wooden spoon, until the polenta is cooked and it starts to pull away from the sides of the saucepan. Pour the polenta into the prepared dish and spread evenly. Let cool completely.

For the mushroom ragù: In a skillet, heat the olive oil over medium heat. Add the garlic and sauté until fragrant. Add the mushrooms and sauté until tender and most of the liquid has evaporated. Season with salt and pepper and keep warm.

For the fontina sauce: In a saucepan, melt the butter over medium heat. Whisk in the flour and cook until bubbly. Whisk in the milk in a thin stream and simmer, whisking constantly, until the mixture begins to thicken. Remove from heat and stir in the cheese until melted. Season with salt and pepper and keep warm.

In a large nonstick skillet, melt the 3 tablespoons butter over medium heat. Cut the cooled polenta into 6 pieces. Add the polenta to the skillet and cook until lightly browned on both sides. Divide the polenta onto 6 plates. Pour the sauce over and top with the mushrooms. Sprinkle with parsley and serve immediately.

Serves 6
Serve with Sterling Vineyards
Merlot

STONE CREEK
WINERY

Stone Creek's Tasting Room is located in Kenwood in the heart of Sonoma County, in what was once a one-room schoolhouse. This historical building was erected in 1890 and was one of the first public schools in the Los Guilicos Valley. In addition to its colorful history, the "Old Blue Schoolhouse" is now the home of Stone Creek Wines.

APPLE QUESADILLAS

Serve these tasty treats from Marc Downie of Catering by Design as an hors d' oeuvre or evening snack.

6 large flour tortillas

12 ounces Monterey jack cheese, grated

4 ounces Parmesan cheese, grated

1 Granny Smith apple, thinly sliced

1 egg, lightly beaten

2 tablespoons minced cilantro

Preheat oven to 375 degrees F.

Place 3 tortillas on a baking sheet. Divide the Monterey jack cheese on top of the tortillas. Place the apple slices on top of the Monterey jack. Divide the Parmesan on top of the apples. Place the remaining tortillas on top and press gently. Brush the tops with the egg and sprinkle with cilantro. Bake for about 10 minutes, or until the cheese starts to melt. Raise the oven temperature to broil, and broil just until the tops turn golden brown. Remove from oven and cool slightly before slicing into wedges. Serve immediately.

Serves 6 to 8
Serve with Stone Creek Winery
Sauvignon Blanc

RUSSIAN RIVER
VINEYARDS

1997
CALIFORNIA
ECO-ZIN
ZINFANDEL

TOPOLOS RUSSIAN RIVER VINEYARDS

Topolos Russian River Vineyards is a family-owned winery and restaurant in Sonoma County just an hour north of San Francisco and fifteen minutes west of Santa Rosa. Whether you choose to dine outside around the fountain patio or inside by the fireplace, Russian River Vineyards is the ultimate Sonoma County winery experience. The ambience is casual but elegant, and the menus combine authentic Greek cuisine from the Topolos family's recipes with offerings from the rest of the Mediterranean and the chef's creative inventions.

WINTER VEGETABLE SOUP
with Scotch Whisky

The smoky undertones of the scotch whisky in this medley of vegetables, from chef Bob Engle, highlights the barrel tones of the Topolos Zinfandel.

3 tablespoons butter

1 onion, peeled and chopped

1 carrot, peeled and chopped

1 parsnip, peeled and chopped

1 potato, peeled and chopped

1 rutabaga, peeled and chopped

1 turnip, peeled and chopped

3 cups vegetable stock

1 teaspoon minced fresh thyme

3/4 teaspoon salt

1/4 teaspoon freshly ground black pepper

1/4 teaspoon Worcestershire sauce

3/4 cup heavy cream

3 tablespoons Scotch whisky

(recipe continued on next page)

🍃 In a large pot, melt the butter over medium heat. Add the onion and sauté until translucent. Add the carrot, parsnip, potato, rutabaga, and turnip and sauté for about 10 minutes, or until lightly golden. Stir in the vegetable stock, thyme, salt, pepper, and Worcestershire sauce and bring to a simmer. Cover the pot, reduce heat to medium-low, and simmer for 45 minutes, or until the vegetables are very tender. Purée in batches in a blender, then return to the pot. Stir in the cream and whisky and heat through.

Serves 6
Serve with Topolos Russian River Vineyards Zinfandel

If God forbade drinking would he have made wine so good?
Cardinal Richelieu

TREFETHEN VINEYARDS

*Tradition combines with technology at Trefethen Vineyards,
where a century-old winery and the latest in winemaking
equipment give the Trefethen family, and their wines, the best
of both worlds. First planted to grapes in the 1850s, the Eshcol ranch, as it was known back then, received its name from
a biblical allusion to an immense cluster of grapes. In 1968,
Gene and Katie Trefethen revitalized the old Eshcol property
and planted new vines on the 600-acre valley estate and on
50-acres to the northwest. The first wines were vinified in
1973, and today wine production has climbed to 75,000
cases per year. The Trefethen family has this to say about
their wines: "Winemaking is part agriculture and part par-
enting. We are proud to introduce you to what we have wor-
ried over and cared for—our wines. They are meant to be
shared and enjoyed among friends."*

POTATO SALAD
with Zucchini, Peppers & Spinach Dressing

This summer salad is one of Janet Trefethen's famous specialties from her garden.

SPINACH DRESSING:

10 ounces baby spinach

1/3 cup red wine vinegar

1 tablespoon Dijon mustard

1 cup olive oil

Salt and freshly ground black pepper to taste

3 pounds red potatoes

3 zucchini, julienned

1 roasted red bell pepper, peeled and diced

1/3 cup sliced scallions

3 tablespoons chopped fresh tarragon

Salt and freshly ground black pepper to taste

For the dressing: In a large skillet, sauté the spinach over medium-low heat until wilted. Place the spinach in the bowl of a food processor and add the vinegar and mustard. Process until smooth. With the motor running, add the olive oil in a thin stream until all is incorporated. Season with salt and pepper. Pour the dressing into a large bowl.

Steam the potatoes just until tender. Peel and cut into $1/2$-inch cubes. Place the hot potatoes in the bowl with the dressing and toss to coat. Steam the zucchini until tender, then add to the potatoes. Add the bell pepper, scallions, and tarragon and toss to coat. Season with salt and pepper. Serve at room temperature.

Serves 6
Serve with Trefethen Vineyards
Chardonnay

of a total of 33,879 Bottles

Est. 1885

ESTATE BOTTLED

CARSI VINEYARD
Barrel Fermented
NAPA VALLEY

Chardonnay

PRODUCED AND BOTTLED BY

ST. HELENA, CALIFORNIA

ALCOHOL 13% BY VOLUME   CONTAINS SULFITES

V. SATTUI WINERY

V. Sattui Winery is a family-owned winery established in 1885 and located in St. Helena, the very heart of California's famous Napa Valley. Their award-winning wines are sold exclusively at the winery, by mail order, and from their website direct to customers. Surrounding the beautiful stone winery is a large tree-shaded picnic ground. V. Sattui also boasts a large gourmet cheese shop and deli.

SUNCHOKE &
POTATO GRATIN

*Sunchokes, also known as Jerusalem
artichokes, take front stage in this intensely
flavorful gratin.*

1 pound sunchokes, scrubbed and thinly sliced

1 pound Yukon Gold potatoes, peeled and
    thinly sliced

¼ cup V. Sattui Winery Chardonnay

¼ cup olive oil

3 cloves garlic, minced

1 teaspoon minced fresh thyme

Salt and freshly ground black pepper to taste

½ cup freshly grated Parmesan cheese

❦ Preheat oven to 350 degrees F. Oil a 2-quart
baking dish with a lid.

(recipe continued on next page)

Alternately layer the sliced sunchokes and potatoes in the prepared baking dish. In a small bowl, stir together the wine, olive oil, garlic, thyme, salt, and pepper. Pour the mixture over the potatoes and sunchokes. Sprinkle with the Parmesan cheese. Cover the dish and bake 30 minutes. Remove the lid and bake an additional 30 minutes, or until the potatoes and sunchokes are very tender and the liquid has been absorbed. Serve immediately.

Serves 6
Serve with V. Sattui Winery
Chardonnay

There is no gladness
without wine.
Talmud

Chardonnay

VALLEY OF THE MOON
WINERY AND VINEYARDS

Embracing the traditions of one of the world's most famous winegrowing areas, Sonoma County, the creation of the Valley of the Moon wines begins with hand selecting the absolute highest-quality fruit available from their organically farmed estate vineyards and those of a select few growers in Sonoma. The winery's vineyards are planted on the well-drained, rocky, red volcanic soil characteristic of the southern Sonoma Valley. The vineyards enjoy a banana belt-type microclimate, producing traditional varietals that include old-vine Zinfandel, Syrah, and Sangiovese grapes with intense colors and flavors.

BAKED PORTABELLA MUSHROOMS
with Goat Cheese

Linda Kittler, my dear friend and the executive chef at Valley of the Moon Winery, loaned us one of her signature dishes for this book.

1/2 cup olive oil

1 tablespoon marjoram

1 tablespoon rosemary

1 tablespoon thyme

1 teaspoon freshly ground black pepper

1 teaspoon coarse salt

6 portabella mushrooms

1/3 cup balsamic vinegar, divided

1 cup crumbled goat cheese

Preheat oven to 400 degrees F. Lightly oil a rimmed baking sheet.

In a small bowl, stir together the olive oil, marjoram, rosemary, thyme, pepper, and salt. Let the mixture stand for 15 minutes to allow the flavors to marry.

With a small sharp knife, carefully remove the tough stems from the mushrooms and discard. Brush the mushrooms with the olive oil mixture. Place the mushrooms, gill side down, on the prepared baking sheet. Bake for 4 minutes. Turn the mushrooms over and drizzle with the balsamic vinegar. Bake an additional 3 minutes. Divide the cheese on top of the mushrooms and bake an additional 4 minutes, or until the cheese is lightly browned. Serve immediately.

Serves 6
Serve with Valley of the Moon Winery and Vineyards Zinfandel

THE WINERIES:

Arrowood Vineyards & Winery
14347 Sonoma Highway
Glen Ellen, CA 95442
707.938.5170

Atlas Peak Vineyards
3700 Soda Canyon Road
Napa, CA 94581
707.252.7971

Beaulieu Vineyard
1960 St. Helena Highway
Rutherford, CA 94573
707.963.2411

Belvedere Vineyards and Winery
435 West Dry Creek Road
Healdsburg, CA 95448
707.433.8236

Benziger Family Winery
1883 London Ranch Road
Glen Ellen, CA 95442
707.935.3000

Buena Vista Carneros
18000 Old Winery Road
Sonoma, CA 95476
800.926.1266

Canyon Road Winery
19550 Geyserville Avenue
Geyserville, CA 95441
707.857.3417

Cardinale
Post Office Box 328
Oakville, CA 94562
707.944.2807

Chateau Montelena Winery
1429 Tubbs Lane
Calistoga, CA 94515
707.942.5105

De Loach Vineyards
1791 Olivet Road
Santa Rosa, CA 95401
707.526.9111

Domaine Carneros
1240 Duhig Road
Napa, CA 94559
707.257.3020

Dry Creek Vineyard
3770 Lambert Bridge Road
Healdsburg, CA 95448
707.433.1000

Duckhorn Vineyards
1000 Lodi Lane
St. Helena, CA 94574
707.963.7108

Ferrari-Carano Winery
8761 Dry Creek Road
Healdsburg, CA 95448
707.433.6700

Fetzer Vineyards
13601 Eastside Road
Hopland, CA 95449
707.744.7600

Frey Vineyards
14000 Tomki Road
Redwood Valley, CA 95470
707.485.5177

Geyser Peak Winery
22281 Chianti Road
Geyserville, CA 95441
707.857.9463

Glen Ellen Winery
14301 Arnold Drive
Glen Ellen, CA 95442
707.939.6277

Gloria Ferrer Champagne Caves
23555 Highway 121
Sonoma, CA 95476
707.996.7256

Husch Vineyards
4400 Highway 128
Philo, CA 95466
707.462.5370

Kendall-Jackson Wine Center
5007 Fulton Road
Santa Rosa, CA 95439
707.571.8100

Kenwood Vineyards and Winery
9592 Sonoma Highway
Kenwood, CA 95452
707.833.5891

Korbel Champagne Cellars
13250 River Road
Guerneville, CA 95446
707.824.7000

La Crema
3690 Laughlin Road
Windsor, CA 95492
707.571.1504

Ledson Vineyards and Winery
7335 Sonoma Highway
Kenwood, CA 95452
707.833.2330

Louis M. Martini Winery
254 South St. Helena Highway
St. Helena, CA 94574
707.963.2736

Markham Vineyards
2812 St. Helena Highway
St. Helena, CA 94574
707.963.5292

Mumm Cuvée Napa
8445 Silverado Trail
Rutherford, CA 94573
707.942.3434

Oakville Ranch Vineyards
   and Winery
7850 Silverado Trail
Oakville, CA 94562
707.944.9500

Parducci Wine Estates
501 Parducci Road
Ukiah, CA 95482
707.463.5350

Peju Province
8466 St. Helena Highway
Rutherford, CA 94573
707.963.3600

Robert Mondavi Winery
7801 St. Helena Highway
Oakville, CA 94562
707.226.1395

Rodney Strong Vineyards
11455 Old Redwood Highway
Healdsburg, CA 95448
707.433.6521

Sterling Vineyards
1111 Dunaweal Lane
Calistoga, CA 94515
707.942.3300

Stone Creek Winery
9380 Sonoma Highway
Kenwood, CA 95452
707.833.4455

Storybook Mountain Vineyards
3835 Highway 128
Calistoga, CA 94515
707.942.5310

Topolos at Russian River
5700 Gravenstien Highway, North
Forestville, CA 95436
707.887.1575

Trefethen Vineyards
1160 Oak Knoll Avenue
Napa, CA 94558
707.255.7700

V. Sattui Winery
1111 White Lane
St. Helena, CA 94574
707.963.7774

Valley of the Moon Winery
777 Madrone Road
Glen Ellen, CA 95442
707.996.6941

THE CATERERS:

Catering by Design
Post Office Box 1866
Glen Ellen, CA 95442
707.935.0390

Linda Thomas Catering
Napa Valley, CA
707.944.8096

Patricia Caringella Catering
Lake Oswego, OR
503.636.2952

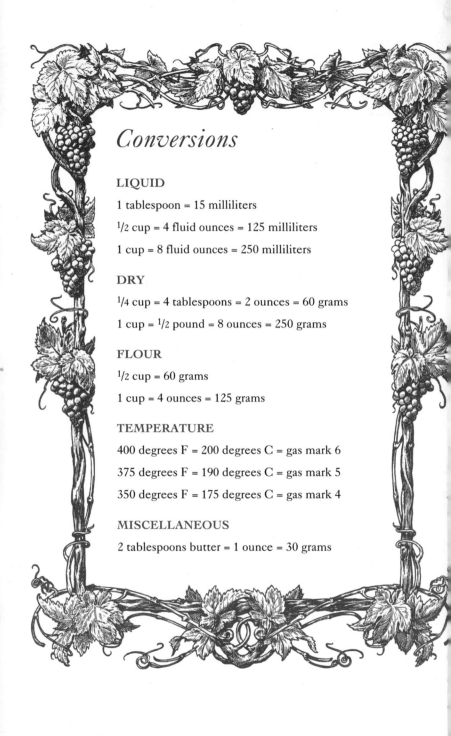

Conversions

LIQUID

1 tablespoon = 15 milliliters

1/2 cup = 4 fluid ounces = 125 milliliters

1 cup = 8 fluid ounces = 250 milliliters

DRY

1/4 cup = 4 tablespoons = 2 ounces = 60 grams

1 cup = 1/2 pound = 8 ounces = 250 grams

FLOUR

1/2 cup = 60 grams

1 cup = 4 ounces = 125 grams

TEMPERATURE

400 degrees F = 200 degrees C = gas mark 6

375 degrees F = 190 degrees C = gas mark 5

350 degrees F = 175 degrees C = gas mark 4

MISCELLANEOUS

2 tablespoons butter = 1 ounce = 30 grams